How to Engage Youth to Drive Corporate Sustainability

Roles and Interventions

Nicolò Wojewoda

e: nicolo.wojewoda@gmail.com

w: http://nicolowojewoda.com

t: @nwoje

f: http://www.facebook.com/nicolo.wojewoda

l: http://www.linkedin.com/in/nwojewoda

First published in 2013 by Dō Sustainability

87 Lonsdale Road, Oxford OX2 7ET, UK

ISBN 978-1-909293-49-6 (eBook-ePub)

ISBN 978-1-909293-50-2 (eBook-PDF)

ISBN 978-1-909293-48-9 (Paperback)

A catalogue record for this title is available from the British Library.

Dō Sustainability strives for net positive social and environmental impact. See our sustainability policy at **www.dosustainability.com**.

Page design and typesetting by Alison Rayner

Cover by Becky Chilcott

For further information on Dō Sustainability, visit our website: **www.dosustainability.com**

DōShorts

Dō Sustainability is the publisher of DōShorts: short, high-value ebooks that distil sustainability best practice and business insights for busy, results-driven professionals. Each DōShort can be read in 90 minutes.

New and forthcoming DōShorts – stay up to date

We publish 3 to 5 new DōShorts each month. The best way to keep up to date? Sign up to our short, monthly newsletter. Go to **www.dosustainability.com/newsletter** to sign up to the Dō Newsletter. Some of our latest and forthcoming titles include:

- *Promoting Sustainable Behaviour: A Practical Guide to What Works* Adam Corner
- *Sustainable Transport Fuels Business Briefing* David Thorpe
- *The First 100 Days: Plan, Prioritise & Build a Sustainable Organisation* Anne Augustine
- *Full Product Transparency: Cutting the Fluff Out of Sustainability* Ramon Arratia
- *Making the Most of Standards* Adrian Henriques
- *How to Account for Sustainability: A Business Guide to Measuring and Managing* Laura Musikanski
- *Sustainability in the Public Sector: An Essential Briefing for Stakeholders* Sonja Powell
- *Sustainability Reporting for SMEs: Competitive Advantage Through Transparency* Elaine Cohen
- *REDD+ and Business Sustainability: A Guide to Reversing Deforestation for Forward Thinking Companies* Brian McFarland

- *How Gamification Can Help Your Business Engage in Sustainability* Paula Owen
- *Sustainable Energy Options for Business* Philip Wolfe
- *Adapting to Climate Change: 2.0 Enterprise Risk Management* Mark Trexler & Laura Kosloff

Subscriptions

In addition to individual sales of our ebooks, we now offer subscriptions. Access 60+ ebooks for the price of 5 with a personal subscription to our full e-library. Institutional subscriptions are also available for your staff or students. Visit **www.dosustainability.com/books/subscriptions** or email **veruschka@dosustainability.com**

Write for us, or suggest a DōShort

Please visit **www.dosustainability.com** for our full publishing programme. If you don't find what you need, write for us! Or suggest a DōShort on our website. We look forward to hearing from you.

....

Abstract

THIS BOOK AIMS TO RAISE AWARENESS among business professionals of the value that young people bring to corporate sustainability efforts, in their multiple roles and through a diverse array of interventions. The book also aims at providing practical, specific recommendations that professionals can adopt in their project, department, or widely in the organization, to improve engagement of young people and thus drive forward – with more effectiveness and legitimacy – corporate sustainability efforts. It focuses on three key roles that young people can play: as social customers, future intrapreneurs, and impact partners. For each of these roles, there is a case study illustrating how successful companies or youth organizations have harnessed the energy and talent of young people in that role. Finally, some considerations are outlined on the future of youth engagement in corporate social responsibility (CSR), in consideration of the changing nature of the sustainability space.

About the Author

 **NICOLÒ WOJEWODA** is a global organizer, committed to leaving a more sustainable world as the legacy of his generation. He is currently a climate change campaigner in the European team of 350.org. He has led and initiated youth projects and organizations over the past nine years in Europe and then globally, building meaningful partnerships with non-profit organizations, business leaders, and policy-makers. Recently, he has coordinated a youth-led coalition of 100 partner organizations towards the UN summit on sustainable development, and organized a global consultation to draft a manifesto on democracy and sustainable development. He lives in London, UK.

Acknowledgments

A NUMBER OF PEOPLE HAVE CONTRIBUTED to the development of this book. I want to thank Akhtar Badshah, Alan Frei, Andre Campbell, Andrea Carafa, Andrew Schwartz, Bernadette Fischler, Brett Scott, Cynthia Figge, Dharmesh Mistry, Eliane Khoury, Geoffrey Roe, Gert Jan van den Berg, Halina Ward, Hans J. Hoyer, Ingunn Aanes, John Egan, John Townsend, Justin Goldbach, Jyoti Panday, Kamel Magour, Maëva Tordo, Marli Porth, Monika Mitchell, Monique Simon, Nadina Busuioc, Nancy Smith, Nicole Meier-Heim, Noha Hefny, Nomathemba Shepherd, Paul Klein, Peter Walters, Philipp Schöffmann, Rebecca Sweetman, Rowland Hill, Ursula Fischler-Strasak, Vimbai Gwata, Wiebke Toussaint and Zdeněk Fous for providing contacts, insights, but most of all their precious time to help further my research. If I have inadvertently missed someone from this list, my apologies.

I also want to thank my current employer, 350.org, who provided me with the flexibility necessary to finish the book in the time agreed with the publisher.

Contents

Preface

THE IDEA FOR THIS DŌSHORT came to me in the summer of 2012. I had just returned from one of the largest gatherings of heads of state and government in recent history, the UN Conference on Sustainable Development (also known as *Rio+20*). Nation-states (with notable exceptions) had once again failed to show leadership in the transition to a greener and fairer future. But there were two positive notes, two hopes for the future that I thought could be salvaged from that wreck: business and young people. At Rio de Janeiro, both of them came with real commitments and concrete intentions to further the cause of sustainability: for businesses, out of a sense of responsibility as corporate citizens and perhaps a genuine sense of farsightedness for their own prospects; for young people, out of a moral, but also practical, obligation to take action and shape the world they are and will be living in, for theirs and for future generations alike.

And then it struck me: we often talk about public–private partnerships as collaborations between governments and business, and we often talk about getting young people involved in issues that affect them – often referring to public policy- and decision-making – but shouldn't we talk just as often about getting young people involved in business decisions that affect them, and partnering with business to deliver sustainability?

If you're reading this, you know what my answer to that question is. Far from being a comprehensive overview of reasons, approaches, tools and insights on how to engage young people to drive corporate sustainability, this book is an attempt not just to start, but to ignite the conversation on the subject. Please challenge every single line in the text, just as I imagine I will challenge it myself as I progress in my research and reflection, and share those minor or major objections with me and with the broader community – it's the only way to ensure that conversation can continue and spread.

For businesses, I hope this contributes to delivering more effectively against indicators other than your bottom line, and appreciating young people's role in that journey.

For young people, I hope this gives you a glimpse into the otherwise distant and obscure world of corporate sustainability, and I hope it gives you confidence in approaching this foreign world with renewed resolve. Many companies want to do well *and* do good, and your contribution can help them steer in the right direction.

Good luck to you both. You can count on my help.

CHAPTER 1

Why Engage With Young People?

THERE ARE THREE NUMBERS that, above others, should give you pause for reflection and prompt you to action: 1.2 billion, 92%, 3.

- There are **1.2 billion** young people in the world aged between 15 and 24, making up 17% of the world's population. If we count anybody under 25 years old, that goes up to more than 50% of the world's population.

- Profit as the sole measure of success is rejected by **92%** of Millennials (roughly, the generation born between 1980 and 2000), as recently surveyed by Deloitte. Even more, according to the same survey, over 50% of Millennials believe that the purpose of business is *primarily* innovation and societal development.

- In 2011, a young person's risk of being unemployed was **3** times higher than that of an adult. That ratio translates into youth making up 40% of the world's unemployed. In 2010, a total of 357.7 million young people were not in education, employment, or training – and that number has been increasing ever since.

What we have here is either an incredible opportunity or a daunting risk.

The risk is continuing business as usual, and the quality of young people's livelihoods decreasing, with consequent decline in purchasing power.

Business as usual is exceeding our planetary boundaries, and young people in most of the world are consequently worse off. But increasing wealth will not be enough. The future middle classes will have to radically change their consumption behaviours, in order to adapt to the multiple crises – those are your future consumers, those are the people you will be dealing with in the market.

Prolonged high unemployment among young people risks producing an entire generation of people lacking the confidence and skills to contribute to the workforce. And let's face it, baby-boomers are getting older, they're going to retire soon, and there's a huge void to be filled with talent. How are we going to address that shortage?

Worse yet, a generation largely abandoned by governments, society and the corporate world has resulted, for example in Europe, in not only high unemployment and emigration figures, but stagnation of the economy as a whole. If left untouched, it can become a pandemic with unprecedented cultural and political impact over the next 40 years. And if you're skeptical about the power young people really have over established institutions, when those institutions are allowed to proceed unchecked and without the meaningful involvement of younger generations, you need to look no further than the regime-toppling movements of the Arab Spring.

The opportunity, in all this, is in tapping into that often wasted potential, and investing in young people as a source for good, while that window of opportunity provided by early age is open. Such an investment counters economic and political volatility, and has a tangible impact on young people and businesses themselves. As the former Managing Director of the World Bank, Dr Mamphela Ramphele, once said: 'Young people should be seen as engines of growth rather than a problem to be addressed.' It's not just impact in their livelihoods – it's *leveraged* impact, as investment in their skills and talents will have unquantifiable returns over the rest of their lives and careers. Think also of the fact that young people are not only future leaders of government or business, but potential future investors, regulators of industry, and active in so many other roles that will be crucial to the survival and prosperity of your business.

What comes across through those initial numbers is a key realization: young people (definitions vary) are a massive force to be reckoned with, who are now bearing the brunt of the crises, but who also want to engage meaningfully with business in order to do some good. They are not just digital natives, they're also true sustainability natives. And they're waiting for you to reach out to them.

When researching this book, I've had the opportunity to engage in discussions and listen to the stories of entrepreneurs, executives, academics, and young leaders from all over the world. To all of them, bridging the gap between young people and corporate social responsibility (CSR) efforts required some *social* and a lot of *responsibility*, never forgetting that true sustainable development (which is based on a strong foundation of environmental, social, and economical equity) is an inherently inter-generational challenge, and it is *with* young people – the closest proxies to future generations – that business has the privilege and duty to take the lead.

The general public often perceives CSR as the charitable arm of a company's activities, disconnected from its core operations, and geared towards improving brand image. There's a risk that CSR is being seen only as that. But many companies have sound CSR procedures, and an authentic interest in serving the public good alongside their shareholders' interests. Young people can play a role in fueling that interest, and in better aligning it with the activities that come from it.

This book will present three key roles that young people can play in a meaningful interaction with your business: as social consumers, future intrapreneurs, and impact partners. Each one of those roles will be illustrated by examples that are hopefully the source of inspiration and insight. The final chapters will be devoted to recommendations that apply across all roles, and to considerations about the future of these kinds of approaches.

What I'm hoping to achieve with this short publication is to stimulate a genuine interest in engaging young people through and towards your corporate sustainability efforts, not only because it's good business, but also because it can have an effective impact on the lives of those young people, and on the progress of global sustainability as a whole.

If we need that to happen, we need to break free from some forms of CSR that have seen engagement meaning charity, and young people as peripheral and vulnerable. In those cases, CSR activities become very hard to access from outside stakeholders, like passionate and talented young people, who want instead to collaborate on an equal footing, on concrete impact, playing on their strengths and not on their perceived weaknesses, taking their central place in a company's sustainability efforts. Would you consider peripheral and vulnerable a young green tech entrepreneur in Silicon Valley who seeks collaborations to enhance both businesses' triple bottom line?

And after all, if CSR is recognizing and responding to the interests of a company's stakeholders (as sustainability standard ISO26000 recognizes), it's only natural for young people to have a place in that stakeholder analysis.

Tighter budgets can't be an excuse either: there's a lot to be done with little funding and lots of organizational commitment. And the numbers are once again stacked in young people's favor: they are the largest generation in history, the most educated, connected, and powerful, being able to access knowledge, coordinate action, and collaborate creatively. Let's harness that incredible potential as a force for good.

Summary/What to tell your boss

- There are 1.2 billion young people in the world, many of them are unemployed, and that is putting a strain on our economy and society, with dangerous consequences for long-term economic and political stability if we do nothing about it.

- Young people today are sustainability natives, who are dedicated to companies that do good, and who can exert powerful influence – whether it's on government or business.

- True CSR means taking responsibility towards future generations, and engaging young people as equal and valued stakeholders, partnering with them to drive real impact.

CASE STUDY – Microsoft Youthspark

Background

Microsoft had been doing what they call *corporate citizenship* work for a long time, focusing on under-served communities. When they started evaluating the impact of those efforts, they had a major realization: by stepping back and looking at what the company was doing across the board (that is, not exclusively in their corporate citizenship efforts) they realized that the majority of their focus was on youth. First and foremost, young people were most of their customer base. Second, they were educating themselves in technology, and the company wanted to understand how to help them do that better. And finally, they realized that, especially in under-served communities, young people were falling further and further behind the employment curve. What they came up with, when pulling together all youth-focused initiatives at the company under a common framework and messaging, was 'Youthspark'. I've had the pleasure to talk with Akhtar Badshah, senior director of Global Community Affairs at Microsoft, about the work they're doing.

The initiative

Youthspark is centered on opportunities. The Youthspark Hub is a platform for young people to access resources and realize their potential. Imagine Cup is a business/tech competition for students from all over the world that tackles some of the world's biggest challenges. DreamSpark is a way for students to access Microsoft tools at no cost. Give for Youth is a crowd-funding platform that connects students' ideas with those who can help make them happen. These are only some of the many initiatives, both company-wide but also in specific divisions, with a strong focus on youth – be it those outside of the education system, or those who just came out of college with a computer science degree.

The stories of engagement are many. In a high school in rural Kentucky, where no Microsoft employees could be physically present to deliver training, a student joined in a Youthspark course on programming via video link, and now he's getting straight As and will soon go to college. A kid from a rural village in India has acquired IT skills through a Youthspark program that allowed him to be employed in the capital of his state, in a role that effectively quadrupled his income. And in Egypt, a young woman was elected as a local representative in a small village against all odds, something she says she couldn't have done without the kind of confidence-boosting support she was given in a Youthspark program. Stories like these show that when programs that focus on youth are able to do something, a spark gets lit, and then young people do the rest by themselves.

Challenges and impact

In my conversations with Badshah, some key points emerged that outline some of the complexities and rewards in doing youth engagement work, and that I think exemplify the kind of roles and interventions, pitfalls and recommendations, that will come up in the next chapters:

- Empowering youth is a business driver, but is also a responsible response to a real need in society.

- In a large company like Microsoft, where different programs are implemented at different levels and divisions of the company, buy-in is crucial. The concern some employees will have on their minds is: 'does this have an impact on how we work?' When done correctly, creating an overall framework and messaging for youth engagement in the company as a whole, can have a positive impact on the way different departments work, making it easy for people outside of the company to understand the work it does.

- Numbers add up. From Microsoft employees volunteering to teach computer science classes in the USA, to technology literacy efforts in rural Indian villages, everything can make a difference.

- Young people, if given the opportunity, can become change-makers. Technology has created a level playing field, and if utilized effectively, can help young people create change – be it small, local, big, or global.

- It's necessary to make linkages across the board of a company's operations. There has to be direct responsibility by a specific division, but the ethos and practice of engaging youth needs to be diffused across other divisions. As with broader CSR efforts, they need to be both horizontal (stimulating engagement across divisions) and vertical (allowing a division to have ownership over their own youth-focused CSR efforts) at the same time.

What can we learn?

Before concluding our conversation, Badshah provided some recommendations to other companies if they want to start meaningfully engaging with young people:

1. **Do it, get into it.** You don't have to come up with grand plan. You can start small, but you can start right now, locally and in your community.

2. **Focus on your core competencies.** Don't take action in areas where you're not prepared. Working with what you have allows you to put the full weight of your company's resources (know-how, employees, etc.) behind the effort.

3. **Partner.** Find a local one to work with you, to start with. They often know the area of intervention better than you do.

4. **Learn.** Don't go and believe you have the only solution that could possibly work – believe in an overall approach, but then learn from what is happening as a result of your intervention, and let that inform successive ones.

CHAPTER 2

Who Are Young People Anyway?

AS MUCH AS I'VE TRIED MAKING a compelling case for engaging young people in CSR efforts in this book's first chapter, you may have realized a question remained unanswered: what do you mean exactly when you say 'young people'?

Definitions abound: some of them group young people by age (15 to 25 being a popular bracket), others by particular life conditions (e.g. transition between education and employment), while others simply describe youth as a state of mind, an eternal condition of the soul (and, alas, not of the body). It's not this publication's task to settle on one definition: it's up to you to determine, based on the context and the particular youth engagement activity, what sense each one of them has in its application to your efforts. What I'm more eager to explore in this section, though, is another question. Let me illustrate that by way of example.

If you asked the Chairman of global fashion brand Benetton Group, Alessandro Benetton, what characteristic defines young people nowadays, he would probably answer you with one word: unemployed.

Last year, the group's charitable branch, the *UNHATE Foundation* (most famous for their flagship campaign, *UNHATE*, involving fake pictures of world leaders kissing each other), launched a global communications campaign called *Unemployee of the Year*. The campaign was a publicity effort aimed at turning the stereotype of unemployed young people on its head, fighting 'for their dignity, against indifference and stigma'. But the foundation also put their money where their mouth is, and promoted a global competition where unemployed youth were encouraged to submit projects they were busy with (*non-work*, they called it), and 100 of these projects would be ultimately supported, including financially, by the foundation itself.

Benetton's initiative is not alone in its category. For example, in 2009, The Co-operative Group in the UK launched *Truth about Youth*, aimed at challenging negative perceptions about that age group.

What this kind of effort shows is that more businesses are taking an active role in understanding the young generation, in encouraging their most positive traits, and fighting against (the stereotype of) the negative ones.

Whether or not it's possible and desirable to group young people in a single category (remember: 1.2 billion of them), there's a benefit to understanding better the distinct and valuable contributions they have in the interaction with your business. Negative perceptions, or gross generalizations, can only hurt a reasoned approach to the subject, which necessitates a more keen understanding of the key roles involved in those interactions. Let's take a look at what they are.

2.1 Social customers

With the kind of numbers I pointed to in the introduction, it's no surprise young people can be and often are the largest segment of most businesses' markets. With 87% of young people living in developing countries, there are opportunities both at the Bottom of the Pyramid (BoP) and higher up in the income range.

In India, for example, the average age for a mobile phone buyer has moved to the early 20s rather than late 30s. In China, the one-child policy has produced a generation of young consumers spoiled by so-called 'six pockets' (i.e. two parents and four grandparents), effectively enjoying a staggering amount of purchase power.

And what's more, global surveys report a trend of increasing awareness of a company's social purpose among the general consumer base, so much so that when quality and price are the same, social purpose is the most important factor in the purchasing decision.

Bottom line: there's a huge market of sustainability-savvy customers out there, who can tell real CSR from greenwash; most of them are young people; if you fail to engage them, you lose them to the competition. But watch out: young people can become empowered customers only if they have decent jobs, and only if businesses buy into national equitable growth strategies; remember to meet your future social customers where they are – in the informal sector, out of school, etc.

Digital natives

In addition to their role as customers, young people's social media-savvy has turned them into powerful trend-setters. One tweet going viral, and your brand loses or gains value – what side would you like them to be on? Engaging them meaningfully can result in increased competitiveness and organizational effectiveness.

When I was talking with Cynthia Figge, co-founder and COO of CSRHub, the world's largest CSR and sustainability ratings and information database, she told me the story of an unnamed 14-year-old, who decided to boycott the lingerie line PINK after searching the company's information on CSRHub and realizing that some of its products underwent animal testing. While the action itself might not have had a widespread impact, it highlighted how easy it is for young people to access information about your company's sustainability credentials, and take action on them.

Episodes like this point to another key point in young people's interaction with businesses: transparency. Many consumer brands are part of larger corporate groups who set those brands' sustainability guidelines or regulations. In many cases, it becomes hard for the consumer to understand who actually owns a brand. Young people reward those who make it clear. Publish what you pay, what you fund, what you do – then young people will buy into your credentials.

And it's not just direct interactions that can hurt or reward the business – it's contributions by other stakeholders, too. Just last year, after having put pressure on Facebook for 20 months, Greenpeace convinced the social networking giant to *Unfriend Coal* (disclaimer: I have an Unfriend Coal t-shirt), and abandon all coal-based sources of energy generation that powered the company's servers and data centers. What was a crucial part of the advocacy campaign? A viral video and Facebook page. Who was the main audience involved? You can guess: young people.

Building the markets of the future

And finally, it's not just reaching out to a consumer base that's active now, buying your products and services, but it's also about developing that brand awareness that will ultimately contribute to your success when the time for them to become your customers will come.

'Organisations in banking, legal services, and even small marketing agencies are investing in currently economically nonviable markets with the plan that through shared value, we are building ecosystems that in time will provide customers', reported Geoffrey Roe, of CSR, the philanthropic arm of the Al Ahli Holding Group in UAE, who engages with Arab youth to build their skills and widen their horizons and exposure.

What comments like this show is that young people can be allies in spreading your company's gospel, or they can become the worst incarnation of an angel of vengeance. It's up to you to keep on their good side.

Summary/What to tell your boss

- Young people are your customers right now, whether at low or high ranges of the price curve. They are also sustainability-savvy and have a preference for products/services from companies that focus on their social purpose.

- Social media and other digital tools are used powerfully by young people, and can make or break your brand; endorsing or shaming a brand can spread quickly among young people's peers, and can lead to real disengagement from your business (think boycotts, but not only). Transparency pays off.

- Don't focus just on your current customer base, but build your future one, by engaging young people now and raising the awareness of your (sustainable) brand.

CASE STUDY – NIKE's GRID

Background

NIKE's role as a responsible corporate citizen has developed over the years, some might say significantly. Its current vision is 'to help NIKE, Inc. and our consumers thrive in a sustainable economy where people, profit and planet are in balance'. Self-defined lover of purposeful brands, social entrepreneur Andre Campbell, talks about NIKE+ as 'the world's largest running club with an impact on people's health'. It is no surprise, then, that NIKE taps into a youth audience.

The initiative

It is in that spirit that back in 2010 NIKE gave London-based creative agency Wieden+Kennedy a brief aimed at getting young people excited about running. What the agency came up with was not a standard communications campaign per se, but something a bit more innovative: a game. The competition, called GRID, involved running from one part of London to another, dialing in phone boxes across different post codes, and following instructions that would direct them to other phone boxes in the city. Competitors would get rewards for performance (speed, routes, etc.), either as individuals, or as part of a team. The whole experience was illustrated via GRID's website, an interactive visualization of all competitors' journeys through London, and received good press, especially around the dates of the London Marathon, when it was first held. Local artist Tempa T helped further promote the initiative, by producing a track that would motivate participants before the start of their journeys.

What can we learn?

- For starters, NIKE was able to connect with a generation of *digital natives* where they're most comfortable: through technology.

- Running the initiative as a game, instead of a traditional communications effort, contributed to two important factors: interaction (reinforcing the drive for young consumers to engage with brands in a two-way effort), and fun (successful brands are those that excite their young customers, rather than trying to persuade them).

- Most importantly, GRID takes the focus away from the product (running shoes) and puts it on the activity (running). The activity is seen as having meaning and a purpose: be it developing a healthier lifestyle, or discovering the city. By communicating the positive association between the brand and purposeful activities that are part of a young person's individual and community life, NIKE was able to engage meaningfully with young people in London, in a way that strengthened its brand among that particular demographic.

2.2 Future intrapreneurs

Let's face it: many schools and universities are not fully preparing young people for the kind of career they will need, in order to thrive in the workforce in 10 or 20 years from now (let alone 40 or 50). I talked with Maëva Tordo, founder of Blue Factory and NOISE, two small but growing social enterprises that provide students at one of France's top business schools with social innovation skills. Maëva was upset by the school's educational offer: 'it's sad to have intelligent students willing to learn, and only teach them business concepts and skills of the past – but then again, you cannot teach the future with a top-down approach'. So she gathered a group of fellow students to explain to the school how to enhance social innovation in its curriculum; when the school didn't respond adequately, she started a student club to fill that gap. Although only in its start-up phase, and targeting mainly the youngest cohort in the school, the initiative has had a few successes, with young people (first year students!) getting their foot in the door of prospective employers. Maëva concludes by saying: 'we're facing a disruptive moment in the world, so if you can hire students interested in what's next and imagine alternative ways of doing business, they'll be more flexible and able to adapt and react – they'll know how to find information, and they'll be sensitive to what's new'.

For a long time, the question in business has been 'how do we hire the top talent?' I argue that companies should be asking themselves another question instead: 'how do we identify, invest in, and ultimately hire the kind of social innovators that will disrupt our own company's business, but ultimately help it drive to success and sustainability?'

HOW TO ENGAGE YOUTH TO DRIVE CORPORATE SUSTAINABILITY: ROLES AND INTERVENTIONS

The kind of people we're talking about here often go by the name of 'social intrapreneurs'. Think of social entrepeneurs, but embedded in an existing organization – effectively changing the organization to change the world. There are plenty of them, and it's your chance to engage with them. Established organizations recognize that: Ashoka, the leading social entrepreneurship organization in the world (its founder often being credited with having invented the term 'social entrepreneurship') has been stimulating this kind of conversation in the sector for a few years now. Ashoka's John Townsend captures the zeitgeist: 'you can have an MBA *and* change the world'.

And increasingly young people look at a company's values and ethical behavior before applying for a job. Young employees want their company to work for a social purpose.

Small and large players alike are following and encouraging that trend. A similar model to Maëva's organizations can be found on the other side of the Channel: London-based Enfuse Youth provides training on life and career, enabling young people to take action now. 'We're in the business of shifting mindsets', says Andre Campbell, its co-founder. And, being at a more advanced stage of development than its French counterpart, Enfuse Youth can already count 12,000 young people trained in four countries in just three years – with collaborations going all the way to the UK Prime Minister's Office. And businesses are paying attention: Nokia will be partnering with them on a personal brand and career design session expected to run this fall. For organizations like Enfuse Youth, the case for business working together with young people in their sustainability efforts has a very simple rationale: gain insights, source talent, refresh your brand, and participate in a scalable platform.

When intrapreneurs enter the corporate world, the impact can be great. Amy Chen, now director of sales at PepsiCo, launched in 2009 (just a couple of years after her graduation and not a long time after having been at the company) the program *Food for Good*, addressing the issue of students on subsidized school meals who risked having nothing to eat when schools were closed in the summer. She found a supportive environment amongst her colleagues, but she also fought for the project and persuaded everyone from the new hires to the executives, that that was the right move to do. And it was. Now the initiative is the largest summer mobile meal delivery program in the United States.

Bottom line: if you can *sell* the change, even hesitant leaders will accept it because it'll pay off. Whether still students, or early on in their career, young people's intrapreneurial efforts could be an invaluable addition to a company's innovation strategy. If you fail to engage them, they might become the competition!

Try to keep a few things in mind to drive this shift home:

- Be mindful of *what to focus on while hiring*: what kind of skills are you prioritizing? Is the recruiting process itself reflective of the kind of people you want to identify and get on board?

- Reflect on *where you recruit*: what channels you use, and are they the channels that the young people with this profile will use? Are you considering people with experience in certain areas (e.g. non-formal education, startups)? If so, how do you reach out to them effectively?

Summary/What to tell your boss

- Chances are, you're not getting the talent you need to stay ahead in the market. Excellence requires a commitment to innovation. And since we're talking about CSR, what you need is a commitment to social innovation.

- Schools and universities are, for the most, failing at bridging that gap. Youth organizations and intrapreneurs are stepping in. Those are precious pools of talent for you to tap into.

- In order to grab the rewards of those platforms, you need to invest in them, partner with those organizations, and innovate *together* with young people, rather than *through* them.

CASE STUDY – challengefuture

Background

Crowdsourcing innovation is all the rage these days. Popular platforms such as Innocentive and OpenIDEO have shown the power of crowds to solve some of the world's most intractable challenges, or perhaps some that your company has particularly been struggling with. The business models are varied, but what is common is harnessing the energy and talent of people from all over the world in the pursuit of impact-focused solutions. It's called *open innovation*.

The initiative

challengefuture (http://www.challengefuture.org/) is a self-described 'global think-DO tank ... engaging youth in sustainability innovation for tomorrow (THINK) while creating positive impact today (DO)'. Although known for its flagship competitions, the organization engages in other areas of work: a pledge-based system around sustainable lifestyles, a collaboration hub for implementing the ideas around the competition, events where community members get together and engage with other stakeholders, and a kind of incubator that helps scale up successful initiatives coming out of the competition.

challengefuture offers partnership opportunities for businesses who want to lead *co-innovation* and *idea generation* efforts, in collaboration with youth teams from all over the world.

What can we learn?

- Social innovation efforts are taking place in a variety of platforms and contexts, whether or not companies decide to partake. Aligning your efforts with those platforms in those contexts helps you ensure that you'll be reaping some of the benefits.

- Young people have a proven capacity to innovate, especially when there is a social purpose involved. Invest in them to nurture that talent and to pave the way for a possible employment opportunity in your company.

- Aligning your brand with open social innovation platforms

> not only boosts your image as a company that strives for purpose and not just profit, but also one that is dynamic and open to disruption – two characteristics that make it particularly attractive for the kind of young people involved in these platforms.

2.3 Impact partners

When your business is committed to real sustainable development, it is committed to a measureable, concrete, positive impact in a particular area of social, economic, and environmental well-being. Chances are, other stakeholders are as committed (if not more) to impact in that particular area, too. As youth organizations and groups grow in number, capacity, and effectiveness, many of them can become valuable partners in pursuing that impact, in alignment with your values and strategy.

This role is different from the previous two in one fundamental way: you're not (directly) selling more of your products/services, and you're not (directly) ensuring your company's own sustainability by training the next workforce. But collaborating towards the same impact can have incredibly positive effects nonetheless: from brand awareness to credibility and legitimacy in sustainability efforts and (most importantly, if your commitment to sustainability is real) to a real multiplier effect of your efforts towards economic, social, or environmental impact.

Young people are always best engaged when seen as equal and valued stakeholders. This said, in this particular role engagement usually takes the form of partnerships and other collaborations with youth-led groups or organizations, rather than individuals. It's an approach that often (but not necessarily) taps into the older youth demographic, many of whom might already be young professionals in their own right. And it's the approach that, if sustained, can often deliver the most rewarding results.

Professionals in their own right

Think about AIESEC. AIESEC is the world's largest student-run organization, with over 86,000 members in 113 countries. The organization focuses on leadership development, and ranks among its alumni people like Helmut Kohl, former German Chancellor, and Percy Barnevik, CEO of ABB. With a paid, professional staff, AIESEC is ongoing partner with some of the biggest global brands, like Unilever and Ericsson. In the last year of operations alone, it organized almost 100,000 leadership development experiences around the world.

AIESEC is probably a very clear example, but not the only one, of how professional the world of youth-led organizations has become. A world that often, if you take a look at organizational structures, values, and strategies, retains the defining characteristics of youth: energetic, dynamic, purpose-driven. There are no half-baked efforts if you want your partnership to be successful – only the integrity of your values and your practices (a recurring theme across the three roles) and the excellence of your efforts can reap rewards for you and the partnering youth-led organization.

Or think about the Scouts and scouting, one of the world's largest movements on sustainable lifestyles: a model of adult–youth collaborations, and of empowering young people from a very early age, to deliver value in non-formal education and beyond.

Summary/What to tell your boss

- There are many other organizations working in the areas of impact covered by your CSR work. Chances are, some or many of them are youth-led.

- Even if there's no direct return, it's worth partnering with those organizations, to ensure a multiplier effect on the impact you and the organization are looking for. Also, there might be other benefits of doing that, down the line.

- Many youth-led organizations nowadays are as professional as other stakeholders in different age groups. Recognize and align your efforts with that professionalism, while still valuing what makes those organizations *youth*.

CASE STUDY – Young Enterprise Switzerland

Background

Junior Achievement is a non-profit organization that brings the real world to students through a hands-on curriculum delivered by a trained classroom volunteer. Its Swiss chapter is called Young Enterprise Switzerland. Established in 1999, the organization is run by 16 young people who oversee relations with businesses, with volunteers, and who provide general support to its operations. The organization has now grown to having 17 corporate partners, with successes including attracting investment in the same program from two competitors in the same market (e.g. Credit Suisse and UBS) where exclusivity contracts are more commonplace instead.

The initiative

Young Enterprise Switzerland's program connects businesses with young people. Their aim is to educate young people to be ready for the world we live in, giving them employability skills, building their self-confidence, and equipping them for a thriving career. The alumni of the program give back as volunteers, supporting the next generation and creating a link between their current business experience and young people's expectations and background. Businesses who are partnering with the program interact with it in two different ways: they send their employees – after training by Young Enterprise Switzerland – to primary and middle schools across the country, to present to the kids a particular perspective on their future careers; and they also invest financially in Young Enterprise Switzerland to give more advanced training (with or without the businesses' involvement) to high school students.

What can we learn?

- Donations are not everything. Take a look at your company resources, its expertise and staff time, and think of how you can contribute those in a way that creates positive impact in areas of common interest for you and the youth organization you're partnering with.

- Take advantage of your employees' motivation to share their good experience in your company, and in the industry as a whole. Audiences of young people (or sometimes even younger kids) can be challenging, but ultimately very rewarding if your employees believe they can ignite a spark in them that will set them on the right path in their careers.

- There's no such thing as competition when you work towards impact. Collaborations that increase a program's effectiveness are, even when unlikely, beneficial to the cause. Acting like a team player can also bring dividends in young people's awareness of your brand and your company's work ethic.

CHAPTER 3

Youth Engagement – How To Do It Right

YOUNG PEOPLE'S ENGAGEMENT in your company's sustainability efforts is not limited to the three roles I have presented. The roles may overlap, and there might be new ones I have failed to consider. What I hope to outline in this final section is, regardless of the role, a set of approaches or interventions that you can make part of your toolbox, when embarking on a youth engagement effort.

As a general principle, interventions usually center on mechanisms for empowerment. You're more successful when you co-lead with young people, or let them take the lead. You're less successful when you're patronizing or tokenistic. When young people are empowered and excited about their interaction with your business, the quality of the interaction benefits as a result, in ways that it's hard, if not impossible, to capture in a return on investment (ROI) formulation, or in a strategic plan.

That is not to say that all interventions require a significant commitment of young people's time, or that in every engagement effort you're supposed to be completely open to young people's input in the way you run it. As with many things, the key is not only in the balance, but also in creating an engagement journey, and allowing for entry points at every step of the journey.

Another factor to keep in mind is that if you're a medium- or large-sized business your CSR efforts will develop at multiple levels and in different divisions: different youth engagement strategies might apply to all those different contexts. Let common sense (and this book) guide you through the ones that might be more successful at each stage.

Also, a question you might now have on your mind is: 'where do I find young people to work with?' Hopefully, the case studies and the examples I outlined throughout the text will shed some light. If not, I invite you to check the reading section at the end of the following chapters.

This said, here are some of the basic tenets of any youth engagement effort.

3.1 Your role

A different return on investment

When developing a youth engagement strategy, and in particular when approaching youth organizations who could become potential partners, don't think of it as a way to provide a quick benefit to your company's bottom line. It sends the wrong signal that you're in there for the money and the money alone. Remember that not everything that can be counted counts, and not everything that counts can be counted. Your accountants would appreciate the distinction. Try to think of it instead in terms of impact. Get your company to determine meaningful ways of measuring that impact and, when working in partnership with young people, support them in developing their own impact indicators, in a way that they relate to (if not overlap with) yours.

Think long term

One of the most frustrating approaches to youth engagement in CSR, my youth contacts reported, is a company's focus on supporting individual, short-term projects. While this might be useful in the initial phases of collaboration, if it doesn't develop into a more long-lasting partnership it makes the youth organization jump from project to project, with different partners, which might not leave enough time to build the backbone of the organization, and may ultimately lead to it either failing to grow, or even closing down. Such an approach stimulates for the youth organization a 'wherever-the-money-is' partnership and fundraising strategy, which won't always result in greater, more meaningful, long-term impact. When it comes to sustainability, then, where often the core challenge is behavioral change on a broad scale, recognize that change doesn't happen overnight. Take longer time frames into account, in order to build meaningful progress, scaling up, and evaluation. And the same approach that applies to youth organizations applies to young individuals as well.

Don't tackle just the symptoms, but work on the root causes as well

It's easy to give funding for a group of young people to participate in a city-wide clean-up effort, perhaps together with employees from your company. It's much harder, but ultimately more impactful, to get the same young people to work on issues of behavior change, public health, unemployment, infrastructure, policy, research and other areas that tackle the problem of waste at a deeper level.

Granted, your involvement in those efforts might be harder to market and might take longer to produce intended results, but genuine sustainability efforts are often like that.

Don't reinvent the wheel

Whatever area of impact you're willing to engage with, chances are, somebody has already been doing similar work for much longer. It's very tempting to consider creating a new project or program: it shows an original contribution, it's easily marketable, and it doesn't require the time-intensive involvement of other stakeholders. But is it always the best thing to do? Perhaps it isn't. Try to see, while exploring that impact area, what other youth organizations operate in the field, and find ways of supporting their existing projects. Help them scale up, and the impact will be much greater.

Fund wisely

Be committed to providing not just targeted project funding but, once your relationship with the youth organization is stronger, core funding as well. It will ensure that the organization will still be there if and when your company leaves (and when it does, helping them strengthen their fundraising capacity would be an invaluable parting gift). As one interviewee for my research said: 'it's not the sexiest story to tell, but it's an important one'. As an example, in 2001 Vodafone funded (with £3 million) youth charity YouthNet, ensuring long-term stability in the finances of the organization, and allowing it to develop to its full potential. And once again, think of young individuals in addition to youth organizations: complement project-based funding with fellowships and other career supporting funding.

Learn young people's stories

Give yourself and your employees a reminder of why you're doing what you're doing, by engaging with young people directly, and listening to their stories. They might steer your company's contribution to a particular area of impact in a different direction, or they might just strengthen the motivation and belief that you're on the right path. Ultimately, we all need to truly connect to others, to find meaning in the work that we do. Get yourself invited to events put together by your youth partners, invite young people to your company for a chat, or simply engage with them through social media.

Co-design CSR projects and strategies with young people

Most young people don't have clear enough information about your business processes to the level needed to contribute innovatively to them, and yet at the same time their insights and talents can truly enhance your CSR agendas if given the right space to flourish. So, instead of seeing that lack of information as an insurmountable challenge, open your company up, and let young people take a look at its inner workings. You will ensure a greater commitment to your business by young people, and you might end up with a few great ideas as well, ideas that will drive better impact.

Be inclusive

Unfortunately, it's easy to be exclusive. Young people who might most likely engage with your efforts are those who have the time, the capacity, and the opportunity to do so. Chances are, they're a small subgroup of what could otherwise be your overall youth engagement base. If your company has an equal opportunities policy, why not apply it externally as well, to your CSR efforts? Where are young women? Where are young people with special needs? Where are young people from under-served communities? Remember, you're not engaging them as vulnerable or less able because of a charitable feeling – you're living with the integrity of your CSR approach of stakeholder outreach, you're tapping into the diversity of the youth talent pool you work with, and you're living up to the norms and policies that apply internally to your company anyway.

3.2 Young people's role

None of the interactions with young people or youth organizations outlined here can be considered a panacea for all of your corporate challenges. Some will have no evident impact on your work. Many will fail. And that is not only because of chance and contextual differences, but also because it simply takes two to tango. Being prepared to meaningfully engage young people doesn't result automatically in young people ready to be engaged showing up at your door and sailing smoothly through the initiatives you decide to put them through.

Here are a few things to keep in mind in terms of preparing you to prepare young people for their engagement journey.

Information is power

Quite often, young people will perform basic research in preparation for their interaction with your business. As noted above, that information will often be incomplete and from fewer sources than those you have access to. Given they probably will not yet have had the chance to work in the corporate environment, their research will present a somewhat distorted image of what you're actually doing: an image you'll want to correct right away. Your own sources are a good first step in that direction, but try also to point to experts outside of the business who can help guide young people through the maze: friendly academics, community leaders, communications specialists.

Give young people the opportunity to make mistakes

You need to be ready to face the reality that, although often competent and professional, young people are not the seasoned veterans you would encounter in your other business deals. They can and will grow a lot, in an environment that pushes them to high standards, but is also accepting of their failures and shortcomings. Mistakes are what will allow them to grow, and have an even greater impact with your company and within their lives.

Put them in your shoes

It's very easy for young newcomers to assert ideas over those that have dominated a corporate environment for years, if not decades. You might feel disrespected, or maybe even threatened by this – and you'd rightly become suspicious of anything that young people whom you are so passionately and genuinely trying to engage are bringing up in your interactions. After all, you've been through a lot and they haven't. The easiest way forward is to ignore them and move on. The hardest, but most rewarding, is to try to explain to them what brought you personally and your business as a whole to where you are now (a personal angle does wonders). Don't try to sell them where you are now; they'll think you just want to persuade them – try instead to guide them through years of experience in minutes of conversation. They'll appreciate the effort and you might even win them over.

TOOLBOX – Tools and interventions for engaging young people

Below is a non-exhaustive list that will hopefully inform your decisions on how to engage young people in your CSR efforts:

- **Join boards of youth organizations**
    - Reach out to them through contacts in adult-led community organizations or charities, or through governmental bodies at all levels (whom youth organizations cooperate with, or even are registered through)

- **Establish your company's youth advisory board**
    - Mirror the functions of your regular advisory board, but ensure an all-youth membership, and let young people take the lead of the board themselves

- **Run entrepreneurship competitions**
    - Organize a contest for young entrepreneurs to pitch their idea or business plan, possibly in teams, and over a short amount of time (usually a weekend). Provide

high-level guidance from your employees or others in the industry, and reap the benefits of an empowered, enthusiastic youth crowd!

- **Incubate youth-led initiatives**
  - Either business startups coming from your own in-house entrepreneurship competitions, or those coming from competitions other organizations run (choose wisely whom to partner with)

- **Provide in-kind donations (products, venue space, etc.)**
  - They go a long way, and are a good first step in the ladder of engagement, at often no or very little cost for your business

- **Provide funding (loans, grants, investments)**
  - With the caveats illustrated in the previous sections

- **Do pro bono work for youth organizations**
  - And pick an area of expertise you think you can master

- **Inspire your employees to volunteer their time and skills**
  - They'll become more enthusiastic employees (see case study on Young Enterprise Switzerland)

- **Get your employees as mentors of young innovators**
  - Internalize a relationship that might happen in any case outside of office hours, and try to coordinate and strengthen those efforts

- **Reach out to young people through social media**
  - If you don't have the capacity or skills, find somebody else who can do that on your behalf (somebody with a youth background)
- **Sponsor sustainability-focused awareness campaigns**
  - No greenwashing, just genuine association with causes that align with your work
- **Invite young people to visit your workplace and tell them about your CSR efforts**
  - Everything looks different when you understand its inner workings
- **Set up and maintain an online community**
  - Get a young intern to lead on this and report back
- **Provide (unbiased) learning resources**
  - It'll look less like you're trying to sell them something
- **Invite youth leaders to speak at panels organized by your company**
  - They might not have the expertise, but you'll enjoy greatly a fresh outlook on issues you work with
- **Invite youth leaders to give speeches to your employees**
  - It'll highlight your humility and capacity to learn from anyone

- **Give young people a project/challenge to work on**
  - Either related to your core activities, or outside of them

- **Organize fun activities together with young people**
  - Those are the moments where trust is created!

CHAPTER 4

The Next Frontier

WHAT EMERGES FROM THE CONVERSATIONS behind the examples and insights of this book is a mixed picture. While all of the people I spoke with (whether from youth-led organizations or businesses engaging with youth) seemed to represent a growing trend of meaningful engagement, the balance between the three key roles I identified is strongly favoring the first two (social customers and future intrapreneurs).

In a way, the apparent trend reflects the classic conception of a company's CSR efforts as an additional component to the traditional functioning of a business; in that case, priorities such as preserving or expanding customer base, and ensuring a steady inflow of talent in the company's workforce, are priorities that trump other concerns related to sustainability as a whole (and not narrowly interpreted as a company's own sustainability). It is obvious then, that a greater effort will be made to engage young people as social consumers and future intrapreneurs, the aim being staying ahead in the market. While that might not be an unsustainable position itself, it doesn't necessarily contribute to creating a positive impact in the overall sustainability balance – after all, the core business of some companies (you might even say, industries) is inherently unsustainable, and CSR efforts operating at the fringe of a company's operations will be unlikely to tip the balance away from the negative impact of the core business.

This approach puts disproportionate effort into areas of sustainability that are most linked to that aim – namely economic considerations. Nobody among the corporate representatives I interviewed in my research failed to mention 'unemployment' as a core issue they were addressing with their CSR efforts. But just as strikingly, nobody gave me a single good example of youth engagement focused on environmental considerations.

In a time of deep interconnected crises, it is unwise to try to tackle them in isolation, and it is even more unwise to single out a few of them and forget about the others. With a world headed towards a 4°C increase in global temperatures, environmental concerns must be and remain central in CSR efforts. And young people's contributions to that cause are no less important than their contribution as economic agents (be it as customers, intrapreneurs, or partners). What we tend to see among companies is a strict separation in the CSR sheets: on one hand, engaging stakeholders (including sometimes young people) in communities to further certain social and economic goals, and on the other, tackling environmental concerns in isolation (lowering a company's carbon footprint, greening the supply chain, etc.). Companies and young people must find ways to work together on those issues as well and still fit that into the overall CSR framework.

There is, however, a deeper, newer, and very compelling approach that gives us hope. It calls instead for sustainability 'built in' to a company's core functioning (or 'strategic sustainability'). Whether it's through innovative legal forms, such as B Corps in the USA (shorthand for *benefit corporation*), or through shifting the core business of a company to an inherently sustainable model (such as moving from being a fossil fuel company to a renewable energy one), 'built in' sustainability has impact as its primary aim.

In that new approach, impact is the fundamental driver of the company, and it's much more likely that we'll see impact partnerships prevailing among youth engagement efforts in those cases. The inherent social purpose of corporations will ensure that relatively fewer efforts will need to be carried out to convince young consumers to purchase their products/services, or to convince young graduates to join their ranks.

It is towards this approach that young people should be driving companies, and it is only with this approach that meaningful partnerships between young people and business will thrive, for the benefit of both stakeholders, and the planet as a whole.

Summary/What to tell your boss

- Although more and more companies engage with youth, they often focus on their roles as social customers and future intrapreneurs only, reinforcing the prevalent business paradigm and failing to grasp the full potential of impact partnerships.

- This paradigm overlooks the crucial role of young people in fighting the environmental crisis, and separates youth engagement and environmental concerns in a company's CSR approach.

- A new paradigm, where sustainability is 'built in' to the core functioning of the company, promises to deliver more meaningful impact partnerships with young people, a more balanced approach to all aspects of sustainability (social, economic, environmental), greater rewards with less effort when it comes to expanding the customer base and the talent pool, and ultimately, a greater overall positive footprint on the planet.

CASE STUDY – Pepsico

Background

PepsiCo is positioning itself as strongly committed to CSR – both in its sustainability and stakeholder engagement efforts – with implementations varying according to context (i.e. country of operation). Their corporate philosophy stems from a vision they call 'Performance with Purpose', which includes three pillars of sustainability strategy: human, environmental, and talent sustainability. Human sustainability relates to their portfolio of products; environmental sustainability to, for the most part, water and energy; talent sustainability is about developing a healthy workplace and a good inflow of talent – ultimately giving itself responsibility to develop future generations through skills-building, education, and projects in the communities they live in. The second element of their sustainability philosophy comes from their corporate values – namely, one that focuses on 'care for the community and world we live in'. The third element is their corporate policy of diversity and inclusion (internally and externally).

With such strong premises for stakeholder engagement and sustainability, youth engagement comes quite naturally as a valued approach at the organization, as PepsiCo CSR Manager for Asia, Middle East & Africa, Noha Hefny, tells me in an interview.

The initiatives

As a critical stakeholder (not just for PepsiCo, but for society as a whole), young people are not confined to just one department of the organization; engagement with them assumes different forms and objectives – from health awareness campaigns, to teaching young people how to recycle, to providing scholarships for disadvantaged youth (Noha's most personally rewarding experience and one she's helped create at PepsiCo, focusing on the countries of Jordan and Lebanon).

Most notably, however, PepsiCo has advocated for the establishment of a Youth Forum at the annual Middle East CSR Summit that would allow a two-way dialogue between young people in the region and businesses.

Benefits

The benefit of engaging young people in CSR, Noha explains, is to see a flourishing generation with a positive mindset that will drive the country and the economy forward. By investing in youth, companies invest in a better society and economy in which they'll be operating in the future. Their voices count, and their energy in this way can be directed towards positive impacts in society.

What can we learn?

Noha shared with me some of the recommendations she would give to other companies willing to engage young people in CSR efforts:

- Engage youth as partners, instead of just participants. Get them involved in the planning of your CSR strategy and project, otherwise you're going to tailor a program for young people that doesn't appeal to young people. Give them the lead in some parts of the planning and implementation.

- Talk with them in their language and try to connect with them personally.

- Engage with them, but then focus on empowering them.

- Build trust, believe in them. Only then their full potential can be realised.

- Provide guidance to help their ideas acquire focus – if not, you risk them losing both momentum and interest.

- Be flexible.

- Measure thoroughly the impact and success of the individual initiatives, not of your overall approach. Let your values and strategy guide you, and go where you can make the most impact.

- And finally, never underestimate the power of young people. They are future leaders, but also today's change-makers.

References

1

Global Agenda Councils – Youth Unemployment Visualization 2013
Infographic with key stats about the global youth unemployment crises.
http://www.weforum.org/community/global-agenda-councils/youth-unemployment-visualization-2013

The Millennial Survey – 2011
Survey data on various aspects of young people's attitudes towards business.
http://www.deloitte.com/assets/Dcom-Global/Local%20Assets/Documents/Business%20Society%20documents/Millennial_Survey_2011_web.pdf

How to Engage Sustainability Natives
Introducing the term 'sustainability natives' and illustrating some of young people's attitudes towards CSR.
http://www.triplepundit.com/2012/02/sustainability-natives/

Do Young People Need to Be Saved, or Set Free?
A reminder on focusing on the positives, in interactions with young people.
https://www.ashoka.org/story/do-young-people-need-be-saved-or-set-free

2.1

UNHATE Foundation – Unemployee of the Year
Communications campaign fighting the stigma of young unemployed people.
http://unhate.benetton.com/unemployee-of-the-year/

The Co-operative Group – Truth about Youth
An initiative confronting negative perceptions of young people.
http://www.co-operative.coop/join-the-revolution/our-plan/inspiring-young-people/truth-about-youth/

Business Should Focus on Sociality, Not Social 'Media'
Calling for a more meaningful engagement through technology.
http://blogs.hbr.org/haque/2012/12/business_should_focus_on_sociality.html

Young & Ready to Spend: Consumers' Average Age Dips
Key stats and analysis of India's youth market.
http://timesofindia.indiatimes.com/business/india-business/Young-ready-to-spend-Consumers-average-age-dips/articleshow/16430047.cms

Young Chinese Customers
Key stats and analysis of China's youth market.
http://www.udel.edu/fiber/issue3/world/

2.2

Generation Y and the Workplace – Annual Report 2010
Survey data on various aspects of young people's attitudes towards career.
http://www.johnsoncontrols.com/content/dam/WWW/jci/be/global_workplace_innovation/oxygenz/Oxygenz_Report_-_2010.pdf

How Intrapreneurs are Building Better Businesses from the Inside
Compelling examples of successful brands innovating through social intrapreneurs.
http://www.fastcoexist.com/1680995/how-intrapreneurs-are-building-better-businesses-from-the-inside

The People Want Business with a Purpose (Will Social Intrapreneurs Deliver?)
Presenting a compelling case for giving space to and investing in (young) social intrapreneurs as the next drivers of innovation for businesses.
https://www.ashoka.org/story/people-want-business-purpose-will-social-intrapreneurs-deliver

2.3

AIESEC
The world's largest youth organization, providing leadership development opportunities in partnership with global corporations.
http://www.aiesec.org/cms/aiesec/AI/partners/index.html

3

Vodafone Group CSR Report 2000–2001
Including a mention of the £3 million donation that set up UK charity YouthNet.
http://www.vodafone.com/content/dam/vodafone/about/sustainability/reports/2000-01_vodafonecr.pdf

Further Reading

UN – Private Sector Toolkit for Working with Youth

Making the case of working with young people as partners, to further development.

http://social.un.org/youthyear/docs/PrivateSectorKit.pdf

Toyota Eco Youth

Toyota's environmental education and implementation program in Malaysia and Indonesia.

http://www.toyota-global.com/sustainability/corporate_citizenship/ environment/toyota_eco_youth.html

Alliances for Youth: What Works in CSR Partnerships

Case studies and good practices, sourced and analyzed by the International Youth Foundation.

http://www.iyfnet.org/document/1069

Creating Opportunities for Youth in Hospitality

A Hilton partnership with the International Youth Foundation on youth unemployment.

http://news.hiltonworldwide.com/index.cfm/misc/davos-home

Opportunity for Action

A Microsoft partnership with the International Youth Foundation on youth livelihoods.

http://www.iyfnet.org/document/2163

The Youth Effect
A toolkit for decision-makers on engaging with youth.
http://www.youtheffect.org/

Role of Youth Survey
Survey data on various aspects of young people's attitudes towards their role in the world.
http://research.tigweb.org/roleofyouth/Role%20of%20Youth%20Findings.pdf

What Can Young People Bring to Your Business?
Advice from a corporate director.
http://blogs.bis.gov.uk/ukces/2012/08/20/what-can-young-people-bring-to-your-business/

Social Gaming to Social Good – Brands Matter to Youth Market
Interesting analysis of where companies are on youth marketing, and where they should be instead.
http://www.mediapost.com/publications/article/173465/social-gaming-to-social-good-brands-matter-to-you.html#axzz2JUC3alUW

The Social Customer Manifesto
A perfect illustration of many attitudes common to young generations, in their interactions with business.
http://www.socialcustomer.com/

Closing the Gap between Business and Education Survey Report
The findings illustrate the need for activities by youth organizations in the area of employability, such as the efforts by Junior Achievement Young Enterprise.
http://www.ja-ye.eu/pls/apex31mb/f?p=17000:1002:3979091353877923::::P1016_HID_INSTITUTION_ID,P1002_HID_ID:1,9085

2011 Cone/Echo Global CR Opportunity Study

Fascinating study on the perceived role of business in various world markets, when it comes to corporate responsibility.

http://www.echoresearch.com/data/File/pdf/Cone_pdfs/2011%20 Cone_Echo%20Global%20CR%20Opportunity%20Study.pdf

Why Organisations Must Respond to those Making the Case for Change

A compelling argument for nurturing young change-makers.

http://www.guardian.co.uk/sustainable-business/business-change makers-young-entrepreneurs

Feeding Britain's Future – Summary Report

An interesting example of combining skills training with listening to young people's voice to improve the effectiveness of those efforts.

http://www.igd.com/our-expertise/Skills-employment/skills-events/ 11140/Feeding-Britains-Future-summary-report/

Four Ways to Engage More Young People in CSR

Insights and advice for companies who want to improve their effectiveness in reaching young audiences.

http://www.forbes.com/sites/csr/2012/03/29/four-ways-to-engage- more-young-people-in-csr/

Youth Diversity in Canada – An Untapped CSR Resource

Stats and insights on outreach to young people in Canadian companies' CSR efforts.

http://www.slideshare.net/highereye/corporate-social-responsibility- and-youth

'Get Involved' page of Northern Irish Youth Organization Include Youth

A good example of how young people are open to collaborations with

businesses, at all levels of commitment and capacity.
http://includeyouth.org/employability/getinvolved

Global Youth Action Network
One of the largest networks and databases of youth organizations from all over the world.
http://www.youthlink.org/

For Product Safety Concerns and Information please contact our EU
representative GPSR@taylorandfrancis.com
Taylor & Francis Verlag GmbH, Kaufingerstraße 24, 80331 München, Germany

www.ingramcontent.com/pod-product-compliance
Ingram Content Group UK Ltd.
Pitfield, Milton Keynes, MK11 3LW, UK
UKHW040927180425
457613UK00011B/280